西藏
チベット
TIBET

中国旅游出版社
CHINA TRAVEL & TOURISM PRESS

主　　编：龚威健
撰　　文：吴雨初
英　　文：林戊荪
英　　文：张庆年
日　　文：章辉夫
审　　定：董瑞成
责任编辑：龚威健
地图绘制：傅　莉
摄　　影：龚威健
摄　　影：车　钢
摄　　影：祁　云
摄　　影：扎西次登
摄　　影：王建军
摄　　影：李小可
摄　　影：谢新发
摄　　影：卞志武
摄　　影：袁学军
摄　　影：王达军
摄　　影：杨秉政
摄　　影：王玉龙
摄　　影：孙承毅
摄　　影：李　杰
摄　　影：刘伟雄
摄　　影：赵中路
摄　　影：吕玲珑
摄　　影：蒙　紫
摄　　影：谭　明
摄　　影：格　桑
摄　　影：王一丹
摄　　影：徐震时
摄　　影：郭　际
摄　　影：唐念祖
装帧设计：龚威健

目　　录
TABLE OF CONTENTS
目　　次

积雪啊，是那山头戴的帽子，
森林啊，是那山梁穿的衣裳，
白云啊，是那山腰缠的丝带，
江水啊，在那山下奔流欢唱……
这就是高原西藏，
是我可爱的家乡！
——西藏民歌

Oh, the thick snow capping the mountain peaks,
Oh, the dense forests clothing the mountain ridges,
Oh, the white clouds girding the mountain slopes like silk ribbons,
Oh, the rushing rivers singing merrily at the foot of the hills…
This is the Tibetan Plateau, my beloved home!
——Lyrics from a Tibetan folk song

雪はヨー　山がいただく帽子だよ
森はヨー　山がまとった衣裳だよ
雲はヨー　山がつけた帯だよ
川はヨー　ふもとで歌をうたい・・・・・・・
これが高原チベット
われらの愛するふるさと
チベット民謡

④ 飘扬的经幡
The five – colored sutra streamers flying in the wind (the five colors – blue, white, red, yellow and green – represent the sky, the clouds, the raging fire, the earth and flowing water)

⑤ 阿里神山—冈仁波齐(6656 米)

Mount Kangrinboqe (6656 meters) in Ngari, a sacred mountain for Lamaism, Hinduism and two other religions.

⑥ 羊卓雍措
Lake Yamzho Yumco

⑦布达拉宫：始建于公元七世纪，后毁于雷火等患。至十七世纪五世达赖时期，在早期建筑的基础上，重新开始大规模修建，此后历辈达赖均予维修增建，近期又进行了大规模维修。现在的布达拉宫建筑群，占地 41 公顷。宫堡包括红宫、白宫两大部分，13 层，高达117.19 米。建筑气势宏伟，风格奇特，成为西藏的象征。布达拉宫是历代达赖的住锡地，也是西藏政教合一的典型建筑形式。宫内所藏文物浩多，堪称为一座艺术博物馆和文化宝库。

The Potala Palace: Although it was first constructed in the 7th century, the Potala Palace was almost totally destroyed by fire in a thunderstorm. During the rule of the 5th Dalai Lama in the 17th century, large-scale reconstruction began on the original site. Renovation of sorts was carried out by several of the successive Dalai Lamas, but never on a scale as that which took place during the last few years. The present architectural group covers 41 hectares of land and consists chiefly of the 13-storeyed, 117-meter-tall red and white palaces, towering over the city of Lhasa from a mountain top. Its imposing scale and unique style make it the symbol of Tibet. As the official residence of the Dalai Lamas, the Potala Palace was representative of the region's former theocracy. Aside from that, it is also the site of an art museum and a treasure house of historical documents.

⑧ 大昭寺：位于拉萨市旧城中心，始建于公元 647 年，相传为文成公主所建，后又进行了扩建。位于大昭寺入口处的拉萨八廓街，是拉萨朝圣者最集中的地方，同时也是拉萨商业最繁华的地段。

Jokhang Temple: Legend has it that the temple was constructed under the auspices of the Tang Princess Wencheng, who was betrothed to Tibetan King Songtsen Gampo. First built in 674 AD, it was later expanded to its present scale. Situated in the heart of old Lhasa, the temple faces Bakhor Street which has the city's greatest concentration of pilgrims and is its busiest commercial center.

西藏民族成长的地方

HOME OF THE TIBETANS

チベット民族を育ててきたところ

白雪覆盖的群山绵延，碧波荡漾的湖泊棋布；雄奇的山峰像巨大的摇篮，晶莹的湖泊如母亲的乳汁，哺育着这个古老的藏民族的成长。

在西藏高原，绵亘着世界上最为著名的山脉：喜马拉雅山脉耸立于西南，昆仑山脉和喀喇昆仑山脉绵延于西北，冈底斯、唐古拉、念青唐古拉山脉横贯于中部，横断山脉则是它的东部屏障。西藏境内，海拔8000米以上的山峰有6座，海拔7000米以上的有50座，海拔6000米以上的则难计其数。那些终年不化的雪峰与冰川，构成壮丽的群山奇观。如果从空中鸟瞰，西藏大地就像是一片山的海洋，而众山之王，当然是为全世界的登山健儿所朝拜、所追逐的地球之巅——珠穆朗玛峰。

涓涓雪水，汇成纵横交错的江河。雅鲁藏布江，是藏族人民的母亲河，哺育了最早的藏族儿女；金沙江、澜沧江、怒江，则养育出剽悍的康巴群体。在西部和北部地区，更多的则是内流河和季节河，它们汇成大大小小的、星罗棋布的湖泊。在辽阔的高原湖区间，伸展开绿色的草原。西藏人民总是把依山傍水作为最理想的生存环境，作为美好家园的象征。

在这优美而险峻的山水之间，西藏人民以巨大的热情和丰富的想象，创造着自己的生活，创造着自己的文化，并将之溶入中华民族大家庭之中，成为中国西南边疆的一颗明珠。

Snow-capped mountains, range upon range. Clear, blue lakes scattered across the land. Here, surrounded by magnificent peaks and nourished by the bounty of sparkling lakes, the Tibetans, an ancient people, grew and developed.

The Tibetan Plateau contains some of the most famous mountain ranges in the world——the Himalayas to the southwest, the Kunlun and Karakunlun to the northwest, the Gangdise, Tangula and Nyainqen-tangula Ranges that cut across the middle and the Hengduan Mountains rising like a screen to its east. There are six mountain peaks that tower more than 8000 meters above sea level, 50 over 7000 meters and innumerable peaks of over 6000 meters. At the height of them all, of course, is Mount Qomolangma (Mt. Everest, as it's known in the West), the earth's summit, the Mecca of mountaineers throughout the world. These perennially snow-capped mountain peaks and the innumerable glaciers present a splendid panorama. Viewed from the air, Tibet resembles a sea of undulating waves.

Melted snow flows down the mountains, forming a web of rivers. The Yarlungzangbo River basin, which the Tibetans call Mother River, is where the earliest Tibetans were nurtured. The Jinsha, Lancang and Nu Rivers gave rise to the robust Kamba people. In the western and northern parts of the region are many inland and seasonal rivers which come together to form countless big and small lakes, shimmering like so many stars in the sky. Between these highland lakes lie vast expanses of green pastureland. Tibetans believe that making their homes at the foot of a mountain and by a river is the most ideal choice.

Here, in the midst of these magnificent mountains and beautiful rivers, the Tibetan people have created a lifestyle and culture which are singular but consonant with that of the big family of the Chinese nation, making Tibet a shining pearl in Southwest China's border region.

雪をいただく群山、青い水をたたえた大小湖泊が大きな揺籃、母の乳のようになって、チベット民族を育ててきた。

チベット高原、ここには多くの大山脈が走り、西南には世界的に有名なヒマラヤ山脈、西北にはクンルン山脈、カラコラム山脈、中部にはガンディセ山脈、タングラ山脈、ニェンチェンタングラ山脈、東には横断山脈がある。チベットには、海抜8000メートル以上の高峰が6、海拔7000メートル以上の峰が50あり、海拔6000以上の峰は数え切れない。万年雪をいただく高峰と氷河が奇観を展開する。空から見たチベット大地はまさしく山の大海原。山の王者は何といっても世界の登山家のあこがれの世界の最高峰——チョモランマ峰（英語名エベレスト）である。

山々の雪がとけた水が多くの川をつくっている。ヤルツァンポ川はチベット民族の母なる川で、最もはやくチベット人を育てた。金沙江、瀾滄江、怒江は身体の丈夫なカンバ群体を育てた。西部と北部には多くの内流川や季節川があり、それらがさまざまな湖泊を生み出し、広大な高原の湖の周辺には草原がひろがっている。チベット民族は、山を、川を、理想的な生存環境とし、ふるさとのシンボルとしている。

この美しく、険しい山と川のそばで、チベット民族は大きな情熱と豊かな想像力をもって、みずからの生活と文化を創り出し、中華民族の大家庭の一員となり、中国西南部でうるわしい未来を築きつつある。

⑨ 高原晓月
Daybreak on a mountain peak

⑩ 珠穆朗玛峰：喜马拉雅山脉的主峰珠穆朗玛峰，位于西藏定日县境内，海拔8848.13米，是世界第一高峰，被科学家称为“世界第三级”，在藏族人民的传说中，珠峰被称为“祥寿神女”，是至高无上、至洁无瑕的象征。

Mount Qomolangma (also known in the West as Mt. Everest): At 8848.13 meters above sea level, it is the main peak of the Himalayan Mountain Range and the highest peak in the world. Located in Tingri County, it is regarded by Tibetans as the most sublime and the purest of all things on earth and referred to in Tibetan folklore as the goddess of auspiciousness and longevity.

⑪ 珠穆朗玛峰冰洞
A view of the summit from an ice cave

⑫冈仁波齐峰：横贯于昆仑山脉与喜马拉雅山脉中间的冈底斯山脉的主峰——冈仁波齐，是西藏著名的“神山”。它坐落于阿里地区普兰县境内，海拔 6714 米。因传说此山为神灵之所在，佛教各教派信徒莫不以来此朝拜为终生之愿。

Mt.Kangrinboqi: Noted as a sacred mountain, it is the highest peak of the Gangdise Mountain Range, which runs between the Kunlun and Himalaya Mountains. Towering 6714 meters in Burang County in the Ngari Area, it draws pilgrims from believers of four religions.

⑬ 卓奥友峰(8201 米)
Mount Qowowuyag(8201 m.)

⑭ 南迦巴瓦峰（7788 米）
Mount Namjagbarwa（7788 m.）

⑮ 纯净的世界

A few dashes of snow in an open field

⑯ 大漠冬日
Winter is windy in Ngari

⑰ 高山积水
A nameless lake

⑱ 绵绵沼泽

Swamp in Nagqu, north Tibet

⑭ 辽阔的原野

Flatland in Ngari

⑳ 通往梦幻之乡
Rainbow over a stretch of wasteland

㉑ 牧场晚霞
Grazing cattle and sheep

㉒ 涓涓雪水滋润的草地
Grassland fed by melted snow

23 金色的草原

Pastureland

㉔ 雅鲁藏布江之晨
Morning view of the Yarlung Zangbo, also known as the Mother River of Tibet

㉕ 墨脱藤桥
Rattan bridge in Medog

㉖ 牦牛雄风
The ubiquitous yaks

㉗ 地热喷泉

Geyser in Yamzho Yum

㉘ 玛旁雍错(4588 米)
Mgari's Mapam Yumco(4588 m.), the world's highest lake

㉙ 象泉河
Ngari's Langqen Zangbo, also known as Xiangquan River

㉚ 金沙江从藏东大地流过
The Jinsha River meandering through east Tibet
㉛ 纳木错与念青唐古拉
Lake Nam Co with the Nyainqen - tangula Mountains in the background
㉜ 尼洋河之波
The Nyang River

㉝纳木错的韵律
Lake Nam Co

㉞ 班公湖
Evening sheds its long shadows on Lake Banggong Co

㉟ 措高湖

Lake Conggo

㊱ 高原圣湖
Sacred Mani stone pile by Lake Nam Co

37 茫茫大地
Cattle and sheep grazing in a valley

㊳羊卓雍错：位于山南地区浪卡子县境内，湖面海拔 4441 米，湖水面积 638 平方公里，是喜马拉雅山北麓最大的内陆湖泊。是西藏著名的“神湖”。

Lake Yamzho Yumco: Situated in the Lhoka area, the lake is 638 square kilometers in size, making it the largest lake on the northern slope of the Himalayas. At 4,441 meters above sea level, it is known as the Holy Lake.

阳光和风雪塑造的人们

A PEOPLE SCULPTURED BY SUNSHINE, WIND AND SNOW

陽光と風雪に育てられる人びと

120 多万平方公里的高原大地，分布着从高寒带到亚热带等 6 条垂直气候带，而它的人口只有大约 230 万，是中国人口密度最小的地区。散居在草原、河谷、山间、田野的人们，领略着不同的阳光和风雪，从而形成了有着明显地区特点的生活方式和人文习俗，以至于从他们的语言、气质、发式、服饰、姿态等方面，便能看到赋予他们这一切的家乡的风采。

一切都首先来自太阳的恩赐。西藏的年平均日照时间为 3000 多小时，强烈的紫外线给人以古铜般的色彩，健康而庄重，质朴而威严。强劲的高原风，挟着沙尘与雪粒，世世代代掠过西藏大地，勾勒出高原人有棱有角的轮廓，犹如岁月精心的雕塑，坚韧、沉着、富于个性。

他们站着，就是一组组群雕。

他们在丛林狩猎，在草原游牧，在河谷耕耘，在雪原迁徙，写下了一部既与大自然相适应、又与大自然相抗争的民族文明发展史。走在西藏的每一个农庄和牧村，都能从奔放的牧歌和山歌中，感受到人与自然的和谐，感受到辛勤劳作的愉悦。

自然环境的赐予，生存方式的作用，以及宗教人文的因素，养成了高原人的善良、淳厚和亲情，使平凡宁静的生活充满了诗一般的情意。生生死死，世世代代，在劳动中创造欢乐，在寂寞中寻求宽慰，每一个仪式都郑重其事，每一个年节都载歌载舞。就这样，给高原的岁月以意义，展示着人类最高居所的生命的风采。

This great plateau, more than 1.2 million square kilometers in size, has many localized climates and six vertical climatic belts, ranging from high and frigid to subtropical. Yet its population is only about 2.3 million, making it the least populated region in China. The people vary in their lifestyle and customs according to the environment in which they live—grasslands, river valleys, mountains or plains. One can often tell where they come from by the dialect they speak, their hairdo and headdress, costume, bearing and gestures.

Above all, Tibetans have the blessing of the sun. Tibet's average annual sunshine exceeds 3000 hours. Strong ultra-violet rays give them a bronze complexion, healthy bodies and an air that is at once sedate, solemn and unadorned. Carved by the fierce highland winds, carrying grains of sand and snow, these people resemble groups of sculptures, strong in will and character, product of Nature's painstaking labor.

Tibetans hunt in the forests, graze cattle on the grasslands and farm in the river valleys. The history of their civilization is one of man's struggle to come to terms with Nature. From the popular herdsmen's songs and mountain songs heard in every village, you can sense the harmony that exists between man and Nature, and the joy of the diligent people.

Molded by their environment and the struggle for existence, plus the influence of religion, Tibetans are by nature kind, honest and sincere, which add a poetic touch to their simple, tranquil life. Here, peacefully, people come into this world and take leave of it. With their labor, they make living a joy and in their loneliness, they seek consolation in handling every ritual and ceremony with earnestness and celebrating every festival with song and dance. These are what make life on this, the world's highest human habitat, enchanting and colorful as well as significant.

120余万平方キロの高原には高寒冷帯から亜熱帯まで6つの垂直気候帯がある。土地は広大だが、人口はわずか約230万人、中国で人口密度が最も小さい。人びとは草原、谷間、山間、平原などに散らばって生活し、さまざま異なる陽光と風雪を受けて、それぞれ特色のある生活様式、人文、風格をもっている。かれらの言語、気質、髪型、服飾、スタイルなどを見てもそれがわかる。

これらは何よりもまず太陽の恩恵である。チベットの年間日照時間は平均3000時間をこえ、強い紫外線が人びとの皮膚を古銅色に焼き、頑丈な身体につくりあげる。高原の強い風が砂や雪を巻きあげながらチベット大地に吹きつけ、高原人特有の角ばった顔立ちをつくり、長い年月かけて造った塑像のように、堅忍、沈着で、個性にあふれている。

チベット民族は森で猟をし、草原で放牧し、山間で農耕し、大地で移動し、大自然と溶けこみ、またたたかう民族の文明発展史をつづってきた。チベットのどの農村、牧村に行っても、美しい牧歌、山歌から、人と自然の融和を感じとり、労働の喜びを知ることができる。

自然環境、生活様式、宗教・文化は高原人の善良、純朴、親しみやすい性格を培い、平凡で静かな生活に詩のような情意をあふれさせている。世々代々、労働の喜びにつかり、どの祭りも歌と踊りが欠かせない。このように、高原の歳月に意義をもたせ、最も高い所に住む人類の生命力あふれる姿をかもし出しているのである。

㊴高原魂
A lone yak

(40) 老阿爸的心愿
A devout old pilgrim in Jokhang Temple with his prayer wheel
(41) 康巴汉子
Man from Kamba

42 丰收的女神

Lhoka woman dressed up for the ritual to pray for a good harvest

43 普兰妇女

Woman from Burang

㊹ 小牧民
Little shepherdess
㊺ 提炼酥油
Making yak butter
㊻ 昌都青年
Youth from Chamdo

47 节日盛装
Fantastic headdress for a festival
48 草原牧民
Herdsman

㊾ 辛勤的劳作
Plowing is still a demanding job
㊿ 多彩的田野
The crops look good（farm in Xigaze）
(51) 桃花春色
Peach blossoms

(52) 普兰山寨

A mountain redoubt in Burang County, Ngari

㊿53 一日之计在于晨
Morning in Nyingchi

⑭ 驮着夕阳归来
Returning home after sunset

55 藏北草原
Grassland in northern Tibet

⑯ 马术表演
Demonstrating equestrian skill

(57) 赛马会之夜
Night of the horseracing

⑤⑧ “黑帽舞”宗教舞蹈“羌”中的一个节目

Black – Hat Dance, a segment of the religious Qiang dance

59 牧民舞
Dance of the Herdspeople

60 温馨的生活

Home Sweet Home

㊿61 门 饰
Door decoration

62 世界名犬藏獒与拉萨犬
A pedigree Lhasa dog (front) and a shepherd dog of the Tibetan plateau

⑥③ 西藏婚俗作为一种重要的礼俗，十分繁琐、隆重，亲朋好友以及村人均聚合祝愿庆贺，祝愿新人永远幸福，歌舞宴酒，热闹非凡。

Blessing the newly - weds (Marriage in Tibet is a solemn occasion, celebrated by the entire village as well as by friends and relatives. There are always plenty of dances and drinks, meant to be expressions of good wishes for the couple.)

(64) 堂皇居室
Gorgeous hall, even by Tibetan standard (Lhasa)

⑥⑤ 祈　愿

Turning the prayer wheel

⑥⑥ 朝拜神山

Kowtowing to the Holy Mountain in Ngari.（This pilgrim of the indigenous Ben faith is circling the mountain in a counter－clockwise direction，contrary to the Buddhist practice.）

67 雪野之魂
Manis turn up even in a snowfield
68 山隘玛尼堆祈求行人吉祥、平安。
Mani pile at a mountain pass to pray for traveller's safety and good luck
69 塔 群
Dagobas

⑦⓪ 转经的老人

An old woman takes a rest as she walks round and round a hill carved with images of Buddha

(71) 抛撒风马旗祈祝好运气。
Scattering printed sutra sheets as a way of praying for good fortune

释迦牟尼的信奉者

FOLLOWERS OF SAKYAMUNI

釈迦牟尼を信仰

从公元七世纪起，佛教传入西藏，历经曲折，逐渐演变成本土化的喇嘛教，形成政教合一的统治，直至本世纪五十年代。一千多年来，数以千计的寺庙出现在西藏的土地上。今天，佛教依然为多数藏族人民所信奉，依然是他们的精神家园。

从首府拉萨，到市镇村落，在高山、大湖畔，甚至在珠穆朗玛峰下，到处都闪映着寺庙的金顶。寺庙是供奉圣佛和护法神的所在，是僧人们以其终身探求生命哲学和成佛奥秘的地方，也是信徒们日朝夜拜的地方。在地广人稀的高原，寺庙及其周边，人群最为集中，交往、商业和文化也由此发达。正如到达拉萨的人们从很远就能望见布达拉宫的金顶一样，在西藏的任何一处集镇，寺庙都是最为显赫的，成为一个地方、一个市镇的标志。这些寺庙，是融西藏建筑艺术、绘画艺术、雕塑艺术、音乐艺术于一体的丰碑，聚集了西藏民间世代的财富和珍宝，显示着一个民族的智慧。

喇嘛教在西藏产生广泛影响的奥秘，至今人们仍在探索，但有一个特点是明显的，那就是，它一方面对神职人员强调对宗教哲学的研究——日复一日的诵、年复一年的研析、严而又严的考辩，需要终身不渝、矢志不移；而在另一方面，对信教者则更注重于外在的仪式——永无穷尽的转经、永不停歇的叩首、永远飘飞的经幡、漫无尽头而要用自己的身躯丈量的朝圣路……这一切构成了西藏的宗教奇观，让人不能不惊异于形式的力量。

多少年以来，作为一种已经深深潜入普通人民的生活方式和心灵的宗教感情，那种善良、那种慈悲、那种亲情、那种宽容，成为西藏民族性格的一部分。

Buddhism was introduced into Tibet in the 7th century. After many trials and tribulations, it was gradually transformed into a local religion - Lamaism - and a theocracy came into being which lasted until the 1950s. Over the more than a millennium, thousands of monasteries and temples sprang up on the Tibetan Plateau. Today, the Buddhist faith remains the spiritual prop of most Tibetans.

Everywhere you go in Tibet, from the regional capital Lhasa to the cities, towns and villages, you can see the glittering, golden roofs of monasteries, high on the mountains, even as high up as at the foot of Mount Qomolangma, and by the big lakes. These monasteries contain numerous statues of the Buddha and the guardian deities. They are where monks spend their lives searching for the philosophy of life and the secret of Nirvana and where ordinary believers come to offer their prayers day and night. On this vast, sparsely populated land of Tibet, it is these monasteries and their vicinities that draw the greatest number of people, and it is from here that commerce and culture developed. Just as anyone traveling to Lhasa can see the golden roofs of the Potala Palace from far, far away, so in any town in Tibet, the monastery is always the most illustrious architecture and the place's hallmark. They are the embodiment of Tibet's architectural, painting, sculptural and musical arts merged into one, Their collections of wealth and treasures drawn from the people through the centuries reflect the talents of the Tibetans.

For a long time, people have been searching for the whys and wherefores of Lamaism's widespread and profound influence in Tibet. One cannot help noticing, however, two outstanding features of this faith. On the one hand, there is great stress on the study of the religious doctrines by the monks. Day after day, they recite the sutras. Year after year, they study and analyze the doctrines. Strict rules and requirements are imposed for the debates held regularly among the monks, demanding life-long persistence and faith. On the other hand, lay believers have to perform numerous rituals, including the constant turning of prayer tubes, endless kowtowing before the Buddha and prostrating of the entire body on the ground on long pilgrimages to the temples, the five-color flags which follow them wherever they go… Together, these rituals constitute one of the wonders of Tibet, the power of form never failing to astonish outsiders.

Religion has taken deep roots in the hearts of the Tibetan people, affecting every aspect of their lifestyle, and fostering in them kindness, benevolence, warmth and tolerance. Indeed, devotion to religion has become a part of the Tibetan character.

7世紀にチベットに伝わった仏教は長い曲折を経て、ラマ教となり、政治と合一して、1950年代までチベット地方を治めてきた。1000余年にわたり、数多くの寺院が建てられ、いまでも仏教は大多数のチベット人に信仰され、精神の糧となっている。

チベット自治区の区都ラサをはじめ、村落、高山、湖畔、さらにチョモランマ峰の麓に、金色に輝く寺院が多く点在している。寺院は釈迦牟尼像などを祀り、僧侶や信徒が生命哲学と成仏の道を求める場所となっている。土地が広大で、人が少ない高原で、人が最も多く集まり、交流がおこなわれるのは寺院とその周辺であり、商業、文化もここから始まる。ラサを訪れた人たちがまず目にするのはポタラ宮であるように、チベットのどこでも、最も目につくのは寺院であり、その地方、その町のシンボルとなっている。寺院はチベットの建築、絵画、彫刻、音楽を一体化した芸術の宝庫であり、チベットの民間に代々伝わる芸術品、珍宝を蔵し、民族の知恵を凝集している。

ラマ教がなぜチベットで広い影響力をもっているのかはいまでも探求されているが、その一つの特色ははっきりしている。一方では僧職者が宗教哲学を一生かけて研究しつづけ、他方では信仰者が生涯マニ車をまわし、経文を唱え、地に伏し、五体投地をくりかえし、祈りつづける……これらがチベット宗教の奇観をなし、訪れる人たちはその仏教の形式の威力に驚きを感じる。

長年らい、ふつうの人びとの生活と心に深くとけ込んだ信仰心として、その善良さ、その慈悲深さ、その親しさ、その寛容さがチベット民族の性格の一部をなしている。

72 冥 光

On and on the pilgrim trods

(73) 西藏自治区首府——拉萨

A bird's – eye view of Lhasa, capital of the Tibet Autonomous Region

74 松赞干布，西藏吐蕃王朝的建立者，于公元七世纪第一次将西藏高原的诸多部落统一起来，并建都拉萨，大大推进了西藏的社会发展。

A Statue of Songtsam Gambo (Founder of the Tubo Kingdom, he united, for the first time, the many tribes inhabiting the Tibetan Plateau in the 7th century. It was he, too, who made Lhasa the capital. Both moves helped social progress in Tibet.)

75 文成公主系唐皇室公主，公元七世纪为和亲吐蕃王朝，远嫁西藏赞普松赞干布，留下无数美丽的传说，为后世景仰。

Statue of Princess Wencheng (Still very much worshipped by the Tibetans, this Tang princess was married to Songtsam Gambo during the 7th century to cement ties between Tang and Tubo. Many beautiful legends about her have been passed down through the ages.

76 金色的宫殿
The Potala from a distance

77 从大昭寺望布达拉宫
The Potala viewed from the roof of Jokhang Temple

⑺ 布达拉宫晨霭
The Potala shrouded in morning mist

79 节日之夜
Festival night

⑧⓪ 扎什伦布寺：在后藏重镇日喀则，有一片红白相间的宏伟建筑群，这就是始建于公元 1447 年的扎什伦布寺，是历辈班禅的住锡地。扎什伦布寺占地18.5 公顷，建筑面积近 30 万平方米。

Tashilunpo Monastry: Residence of the Panchen Lamas, it is situated in Xigaze, a major city in the former Zang area. First built in 1447, it is a constellation of red and white buildings. Totalling nearly 400,000 square meters in floor space, the building complex covers an area of 18.5 hectares.

⑧① 白居寺

Palkor Monastery

⑧② 藏王墓位于山南穷结县，公元七世纪至九世纪，吐蕃王朝赞普多葬于此地。

Burial ground of Tubo kings from the 7th to the 9th centuries (situated in Qonggyai County, Lokka)

⑧③ 第五至第九世班禅灵塔

Stupas for the 5th to 9th Panchen Lamas

⑭ 夏鲁寺
Xalu Monastery

⑧⑤ 桑耶寺——西藏第一座佛教寺庙
Samye Monastery, reputed to be the first Buddhist temple ever built in Tibet

⑧⑥ 扎什伦布寺佛像
Statue of Buddha in Tashilunpo Monastery

87 晨诵

Chanting the sutras in the early morning

88 辩 经

Debating a fine point in the Buddhist scriptures

⑧⑨ 法螺声声。
Blowing the conch at a religious ceremony

⑨⓪ 大法会

The Grand Prayer Service

(91) 十世班禅额尔德尼·却吉坚赞在主持火祭
The 10th Bainqen Erdeni (Panchen Lama) officiating at a fire ceremony

(92) **1995**年**12**月**8**日正式坐床的十一世班禅，额尔德尼·坚赞诺布。

The 11th Bainqen Erdeni (Panchen Lama) formally installed on Dec.8, 1995

93 飘飞的祈愿

Flying streamers spreading good wishes all around

⑭ 高　僧
A high lama
⑮ 老　僧
Old monk
⑯ 法会即景
A moment during the Grand Prayer Service

97 僧界仪仗
An ecclesiastical guard of honor

(98) 第十七世噶玛巴活佛伍金占堆·赤列多吉
The 17th Living Buddha Garmabar O'gyain Zham-du Chilai Doje

(99) 僧慈俗亲
Greeting a high priest

(100) 小尼姑
A young nun

(101) 甘丹寺展佛节
Sunning – the – Buddha Festival at Gaindan Monastery

02 哲蚌寺展佛

Sunning the Buddha at Drepung Monastery

⑩③ 跳 神
Sorcerers' Dance
⑩④ 跳 神
Sorcerers' Dance
⑩⑤ 藏 戏
Tibetan opera actor

96 展佛节的祝福

Young lamas throwing tsamba flour into the air from the roof of a monastery at the closing of the Sunning－the－Buddha Festival

⑩⑦ 雍布拉康：雅砻河谷是西藏民族的发祥地。这里，有一座依山而立的古老建筑，这就是藏族的先民们为他们部落的第一代首领——聂赤赞普修建的宫殿：雍布拉康。这也是西藏历史上最早的建筑，其始建年代大约在一千多年前。

Yombulagang: Tibetans say their roots are in the Yarlung Valley. Here, on the slope of a hill, stands an ancient building reputed to be the palace of their first king, Nyatri Tsanpo. Yombulagang, as it's called, is also Tibet's earliest palace building, its age exceeding one millenium.

08 冈巴古堡

Relics of an ancient fort in Kamba County

⑩⑨ 无字的残碑

Legacies of a glorious past – ruins of an ancient monastery

⑪⑩ 干涸的河床

Dried riverbed

⑪⑪ 古格王朝：古格王朝是在西藏地方历史上的动荡岁月中建立的小朝廷，其宫堡从十世纪到十六世纪不断扩建。宫堡遗址占地 18 万平方米，包括诸多佛塔、碉堡、洞穴、暗道和房屋。遗址残留的壁画和石刻等，具有极高的艺术价值。

The Ruins of Guge Kingdom: A local regime established during the turbulent years of Tibet's history, it continued constructing and expanding its palace site between the 10th and the 16th century. The ruins, totalling 180,000 square meters in size, include many stupas, blockhouses, caves, tunnels and houses. The murals and stone sculptures which remain are of exceptionally high artistic value.

(112) 古格王朝遗址

A close-up view of a fortress of the Guge Kingdom

113 古格—历史记忆的深处

The Guge Kingdom, buried deep in memory

⑪⑭ 扎达土林

Spectacular petrified highland basin at Zhada

天赐地予的高原艺术

TIBETAN ART, GIFT OF HEAVEN AND OF EARTH

天地がさずけた高原芸術

正如象征蓝天、白云、红火、绿草、黄土的五色经幡的色彩那么亮丽，在西藏人民的日常生活中，他们对于艺术的想象力和表现力，也是那么大胆、那么强烈。宗教的说教并没有能够窒息人们的创造力，反而给人们表达生活的热情付予了想象的翅膀。从建筑到服饰，从家具到什物，都闪烁着天赐地予的智慧艺术之光。

行走在西藏大地，到处可以感受到艺术的魅力，宗教的和世俗的艺术，生活的和环境的艺术，一种不是为了货币创造因而也不是能以货币来标价的艺术。只有理解了西藏人民的生活方式，才能够领悟，高原的人们为什么把每一个节日都过得那么隆重，把每一个仪式都举行得那么庄严，为什么把一张桌子都雕刻得那么精美绝伦，把一匹骏马都装饰得那么堂皇富丽。

西藏人民和平的劳动和享受生活的热情，本身就是一门别开生面的艺术。

One might say that Tibetan art is as brightly-hued as the five-colored flags that represent blue sky, white clouds, red fire, green grass and yellow earth. Visitors to Tibet are invariably impressed by the local people's power of imagination and boldness of expression in their artistic forms. Religious doctrines have not stifled their creativity. Rather, they have given wings to their imagination. Talent, gifted by Heaven and Earth, shines forth in all their works of art, from architecture to clothing and decorations, from furniture to articles of daily use.

There is an artistic charm that moves you wherever you go on the Tibetan Plateau. The source of this charm is the region's religious and secular art, art that springs from everyday life and from the environment, art that is not made for money's sake and, therefore, cannot be evaluated in terms of money. Only when you really know the lifestyle of the Tibetan people can you appreciate why they greet every festival with such ceremony and take every ritual so seriously, why each piece of furniture is exquisitely carved and every horse beautifully adorned.

Truly, the peaceful labor of the Tibetan people, and the enthusiasm with which they enjoy life, are themselves art of a unique nature.

五色の経幡の色があざやかなように、チベット民族の芸術的想像力と表現力は大胆かつ強烈である。建築物から服飾、家具から日用品まで、どれも天地がさずけた知恵と芸術の光が輝いている。

チベットに足を踏み入れると、いたるところで芸術の魅力にとらわれる。それはカネの尺でははかれない芸術である。チベット民族の生活様式を知れば、それがよくわかる。なぜ祭りがあのように盛大なのか、なぜ仏教儀式があのように荘厳なのか、なぜ一つの机の彫刻があのように精緻なのか、なぜ一匹の馬の飾りがありように美しいのか……。

ポタラ宮　7世紀に造営がはじまり、のちに落雷のため焼失した。17世紀の第5世ダライ・ラマの時代に、宮殿跡に大規模な工事がすすめられて再建され、その後歴代のダライが修理・増築をつづけ、今日の規模となった。最近、また大がかりな修繕がおこなわれた。現在の建築群の敷地面積は41ヘクタール。紅宮と白宮の2部分からなり、13層で、高さは117.19メートル。建築物は壮大で、ユニークな風格を示し、チベットのシンボルとなっている。歴代のダライ・ラマがここに住み、チベットの政教合一の典型的な建築様式をそなえ、宮内には大量の文物が蔵され、芸術博物館・文化の宝庫となっている。

⑮ 大昭寺佛像
Statue of the Buddha in Jokhang Temple
⑯ 佛　像
Statue of the Buddha in a unique seated position
⑰ 佛塔馏金饰
Gold-plated decoration on a Buddhist stupa

118 布达拉宫门饰

Doorway decorations in the Potala Palace

119 石刻经板
Buddhist scriptures carved on stone slabs
120 描金石刻
Gilded relief on stone
121 模制佛像
Moulded Buddha statues

(122) 纪念五世达赖喇嘛圆寂佛事活动壁画

Mural depicting the mourning ceremony at the passing away of the 5th Dalai Lama

123 夏鲁寺壁画

Mural in Xalu Monastery

(124) 古格遗址壁画
A mural found in the ruins of the Guge Kingdom

(25) 昌珠寺珍珠唐卡

Scroll picture made up of thousands of pearls in Changzhug Monastery

(26) 布达拉宫唐卡

***Tangka* in the Potala**

野生动物的天然乐园

WILDLIFE'S NATURAL HABITAT

野生動物の楽園

万里高原上的雪山、草原、森林、湖泊，为各类野生动物构筑了一个世界上最高的天然乐园，为它们提供了天然的庇护。各种珍禽异兽在这里欢乐地嬉戏，在这里自由地繁衍。高原独特的地理气候，形成了许多高原独有的动物品种，有着检高的科学和经济价值。据统计，西藏共有哺乳动物118种，鸟类473种，爬行类49种，两栖类44种，鱼类61种，昆虫2300多种。尤其在人迹罕至的西北部荒原，更是各类动物奔腾飞驰的天堂。

西藏的野生动物大致可分为兽类、鸟类和鱼类。其中，兽类以野牦牛、藏羚羊、藏野驴、盘羊、白唇鹿最为珍贵，鸟类以黑颈鹤、藏雪鸡、藏马鸡、斑头雁、棕头鸥最为珍贵，裂腹鱼则是西藏高原特有的鲤科鱼类。旅行在西北部荒原，不时可以看到成百上千的藏羚羊、藏野驴排列成威武的队伍，与汽车开展赛跑；如果能够有幸来到鸟岛，数万羽鸥鸟展翅飞翔，遮天蔽日，更让人叹为观止。

为保护野生动物资源，西藏自治区人民政府制定了保护野生动物的地方法令，开列了必须严加保护的珍贵动物名单，划列了若干野生动物保护区，使得这些高原财富得到有效的保护。在西藏高原行旅，之所以永远不会感到寂寞，是因为除了那里质朴的人民和丰富的人文景观外，还有那么多野生动物，它们是高原人类亲近的朋友。

The snowy mountains, grasslands, forests and lakes on the Tibetan Plateau provide wildlife with the world's highest natural habitat and the best shelter they can find. Here, rare birds and beasts freely live and multiply. The unique geography and climate have given rise to many animals found nowhere else on earth, and are therefore of great scientific and economic value. Surveys show that there are 118 species of mammals, 473 species of birds, 49 species of reptiles, 44 species of amphibians, 61 species of fish and 2300 species of insects. The wilderness in the northwestern part of Tibet, which few humans have set foot on, is paradise to all kinds of animals.

Among the wildlife in Tibet, the most precious of the beasts are the wild yak, Tibetan antelope, wild donkey, argali and white-lipped deer. Birds include the black-necked crane, the Tibetan snow-pheasant, the Tibetan horse pheasant, the bar-headed goose and the brown-headed gull. As for the schizothorax, it is a kind of carp peculiar to the Tibetan Plateau and considered most rare. Traveling in the northwestern wilderness, you will often find herds of Tibetan antelopes and wild donkeys, in their hundreds, racing against your car. And if you should have the good fortune to visit Birds Island, you will be awed by the sight of tens of thousands of plume-gulls flying overhead, literally blocking out the sun.

To protect the plateau's wildlife resources, the Tibet Autonomous Region government has issued special decrees and listed the rare animals under strict government protection. It has also marked out several wildlife conservations to provide effective shelter for the treasured animals.

The reason you never feel lonely traveling on the Tibetan Plateau is that apart from the friendly and unaffected people you meet and the numerous sights to see, you will frequently have the company of many wild animals, who are close friends of the highland people.

広大な高原上の雪山、草原、森林、湖沼は、野生動物にとっての世界最高地の天然のパラダイスとなっている。さまざまな禽獣がここで自由に生息し、繁殖している。高原独特の地理と気候によって、高原特有の動物がたくさんおり、これらの動物はきわめて高い科学的、経済的価値をもっている。統計によると、チベットには、哺乳類が118種、鳥類が473種、爬虫類が49種、両生類が44種、魚類が61種、昆虫類が2300余種ある。とりわけ人煙まれな西北部の荒原には珍しい野生動物が多い。

チベットの野生動物はおもに獣類、鳥類、魚類に分けられる。そのうち獣類では、野生ヤク、チベット羚羊、チベット野生ロバ、アルガリ（羊の一種）、白唇鹿が珍貴で、鳥類では、クビクロヅル、チベットセッケイ、チベットキジ、斑頭雁、マルガモが珍貴である。裂腹魚はチベット高原特有のコイ科である。西北部の荒原を行くと、群れをなしたチベット羚羊、チベット野生ロバがあちこちで見かけられる。鳥島に行けば、空が黒くなるほど多くの鳥が飛んでいるのを見ることができる。

野生動物資源を保護するため、チベット自治区人民政府は野生動物保護に関する地方法令を定め、保護対象となる珍貴動物リストを作成し、さらにいくつかの野生動物保護区を設け、この高原の動物資源を効果的に保護している。

チベット高原の旅が楽しいのは、そこの素朴な人びとと接し、豊富な人文景観を目のあたりにできるだけでなく、高原の人びととの「友人」である多くの野生動物がいるからでもある。

(128) 西藏棕熊
Tibetan brown bears
(129) 野牦牛
Wild yaks
岩 羊
(130) Bharal (Blue Sheep)

(131) 黑颈鹤
Black－necked cranes
(132) 世界唯一的在冬季孵化的鸟类一胡兀鹫
A kind of griffon vulture, the only bird on earth that hatches its eggs in winter
(133) 藏野驴
Tibetan wild donkeys

(134) 世界唯一的高原鹿类——白唇鹿
White－lipped deer，the world's only plateau deer

(135) 温泉与天鹅
Hot spring and swans
(136) 斑头雁
Bar－headed geese
(137) 生活在海拔 4000－6000 米高山上的雪鸡
Snow pheasants whose habitat is 4,000 to 6,000 meters above sea level
(138) 蓝马鸡
Blue－eared pheasant

139 苞叶雪莲
Saussurea obvallata
140 高原黄杜鹃
Yellow azalea
141 贡山蓟
Cirsium bolooephalum Petrak
142 生长在海拔 5000 米以上的高原点地梅
A kind of grass that grows over 5,000 meters above sea level
143 高原伞形科植物
An umbrella－shaped plant
144 墨脱原始森林中的兰花
Orchids in the virgin forests of Medog

(145) 班公湖鸟岛
Birds Island on Lake Bang Gong Co

(京)新登字 031 号

主　　编:龚威健　英文翻译:林戊荪　责任编辑:龚威健
审　　定:董瑞成　英文翻译:张庆年　地图绘制:傅　莉
撰　　文:吴雨初　日文翻译:章辉夫　装帧设计:龚威健
摄　　影:(按姓氏笔划为序、附图片序号)

扎西次登:②⑨㉓㉝㊹㊺㊻(57)(58)(71)(78)(101)　车　钢:④⑧⑭㉖㉚㊲㊾(62)(68)(72)(88)(89)(90)(91)(93)(94)(95)(98)　卞志武:封面㉟(74)(75)(79)(122)(126)　王达军:⑱㉒㊳(63)(102)　王建军:⑯㉛(61)(70)(108)(109)(112)(113)　王玉龙:(65)(83)(97)(103)(105)(106)(117)　王一丹:(99)　祁　云:⑩⑪(128)(129)(130)(132)(134)(135)(136)(137)(138)(140)(142)(144)　封底　吕玲珑:㉑(54)　刘伟雄:㉙(110)(111)　孙承毅:⑦㊶(55)　李　杰:(69)(104)(127)　李小可:⑮㉜(56)(60)(67)(139)(143)　杨秉政:⑤㊱(96)(114)　赵中路:③(73)(77)　袁学军:⑳㊵㊼(51)(81)　郭　际:⑰　格　桑:(92)　徐震时:(118)　蒙　紫:(76)　唐念祖:㉕　谢新发:㊿(53)(84)(86)(115)(116)(123)(141)　龚威健:⑥⑫⑲㉔㉗㉘㉞㊴㊷㊸㊽(52)(59)(64)(66)(80)(82)(85)(87)(100)(107)(119)(120)(121)(124)(125)(131)(133)(145)　谭　明:⑬

图书在版编目(CIP)数据

西藏/龚威健主编. - 北京:中国旅游出版社,1996.8
ISBN 7 - 5032 - 1316 - 7
Ⅰ.西… Ⅱ.龚… Ⅲ.西藏 - 概况 - 摄影集 Ⅳ.J426.75
中国版本图书馆 CIP 数据核字(96)第 15413 号

中国旅游出版社出版 · 策划编辑室编辑
(北京建国门内大街甲九号)
电话:010-85166715 邮编: 100005
深圳雅昌彩色印刷有限公司制版
东莞新扬印刷有限公司印刷
2005 年 6 月第一版　第四次印刷
开本: 787x1092 毫米　1/12　印张: 10
010800